P9-DCG-302

Space-ology

Looking for Another
EARTH

by Ellen Lawrence

Consultant:
Josh Barker
Space Communications Team
National Space Centre
Leicester, United Kingdom

BEARPORT
PUBLISHING

New York, New York

Credits

Cover, © NASA/Ames/SETI Institute/JPL-Caltech, © Angela Harburn/Shutterstock, and © muratart/Shutterstock; 4T, © BG Smith/Shutterstock; 4B, © Four Oaks/Shutterstock; 5, © NASA; 6, © Yuriy Kulik/Shutterstock; 7, © Orla/Shutterstock; 8T, © European Southern Observatory; 8B, © MAV Drone/Shutterstock; 9, © Elijah Mathews/Creative Commons; 10, © RGB Ventures/Superstock/Alamy; 11, © Detlev Van Ravenswaay/Science Photo Library; 12, © World History Archive/Alamy; 13, © Volodymyr Goinyk/Shutterstock; 14, © NASA; 15, © Angela Harburn/Shutterstock; 15BL, © NASA Ames/JPL-Caltech/T. Pyle; 16, © NASA/MSFC/David Higginbotham/Emmett Given; 17, © NASA; 18, © MasPix/Alamy; 19, © Gary Gerschoff/Getty Images; 20, © Ruby Tuesday Books; 21, © European Southern Observatory; 22L, © Tono Balaguer/Shutterstock; 22R, © tomertu/Shutterstock; 23TL, © Vadim Sadovski/Shutterstock; 23TC, © Dotted Yeti/Shutterstock; 23TR, © shooarts/Shutterstock; 23BL, © NASA Images/Shutterstock; 23BC, © frantic00/Shutterstock; 23BR, © Vadim Sadovski/Shutterstock.

Publisher: Kenn Goin
Senior Editor: Joyce Tavolacci
Creative Director: Spencer Brinker
Photo Researcher: Ruth Owen Books

Library of Congress Cataloging-in-Publication Data

Names: Lawrence, Ellen, 1967– author.
Title: Looking for another Earth / by Ellen Lawrence.
Description: New York, New York : Bearport Publishing, [2019] | Series:
  Space-ology | Includes bibliographical references
  and index. |
Identifiers: LCCN 2018051127 (print) | LCCN 2018051915 (ebook) | ISBN
  9781642802481 (Ebook) | ISBN 9781642801798 (library)
Subjects: LCSH: Extrasolar planets—Juvenile literature. | Life on other
  planets—Juvenile literature. | Planets—Juvenile literature. | Outer
  space—Exploration—Juvenile literature.
Classification: LCC QB820 (ebook) | LCC QB820 .L39 2019 (print) | DDC
  523.2/4—dc23
LC record available at https://lccn.loc.gov/2018051127

Copyright © 2019 Bearport Publishing Company, Inc. All rights reserved. No part of this publication may be reproduced in whole or in part, stored in any retrieval system, or transmitted in any form or by any means, electronic, mechanical, photocopying, recording, or otherwise, without written permission from the publisher.

For more information, write to Bearport Publishing Company, Inc., 45 West 21st Street, Suite 3B, New York, New York 10010. Printed in the United States of America.

10 9 8 7 6 5 4 3 2 1

Contents

A Very Special Planet

Earth is a very special **planet**. Why?

It's covered with water and is home to plants and animals.

Earth, in fact, is the only planet we know of that has living things.

Could there be another planet like Earth somewhere else in space?

Scientists think there are over eight million different kinds of living things on Earth. All of them need water to survive.

Earth

The Solar System

Sun

Earth and seven other planets **orbit** the Sun.

Together with the Sun, these planets make up our solar system.

The Sun is just one of trillions of stars in the **universe**.

Scientists began to wonder if each of these faraway stars also has planets.

If so, could one of the planets be another Earth?

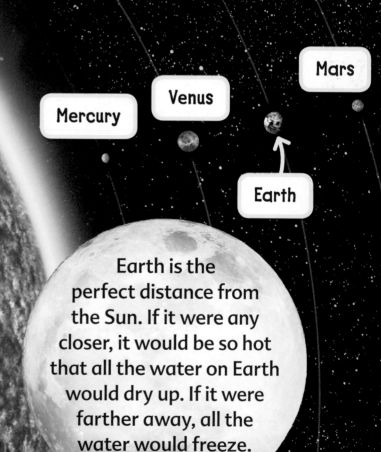

Mercury

Venus

Mars

Earth

Earth is the perfect distance from the Sun. If it were any closer, it would be so hot that all the water on Earth would dry up. If it were farther away, all the water would freeze.

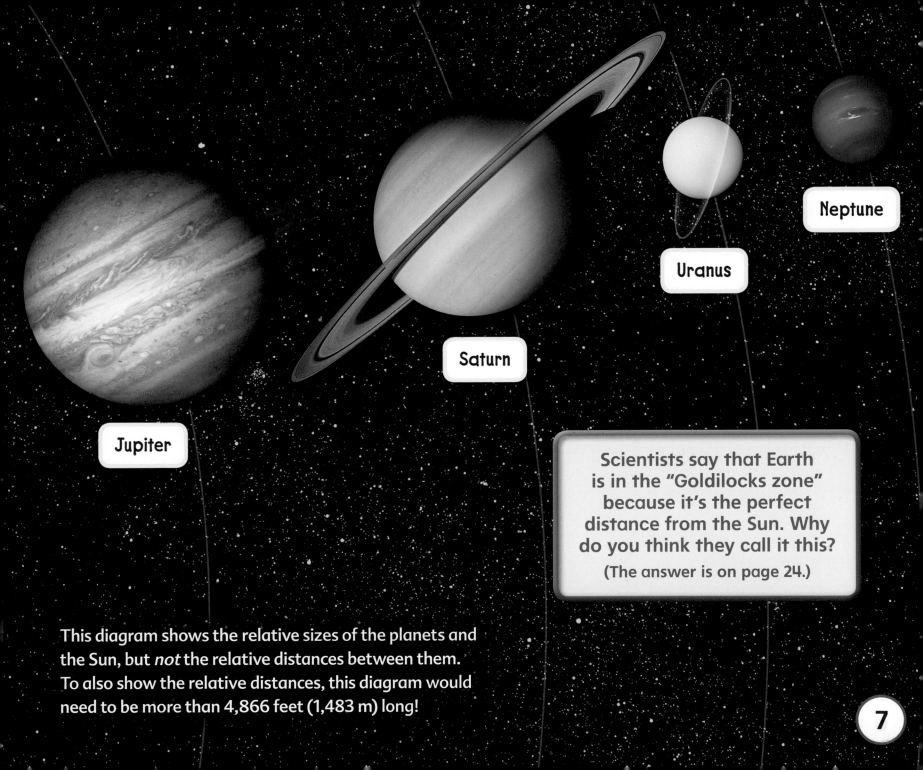

Neptune

Uranus

Saturn

Jupiter

Scientists say that Earth
is in the "Goldilocks zone"
because it's the perfect
distance from the Sun. Why
do you think they call it this?

(The answer is on page 24.)

This diagram shows the relative sizes of the planets and
the Sun, but *not* the relative distances between them.
To also show the relative distances, this diagram would
need to be more than 4,866 feet (1,483 m) long!

A Big Challenge

Stars are massive balls of burning gas that produce light.

From Earth, however, they look like tiny dots—even through powerful **telescopes**.

Planets are many times smaller than stars and don't produce light.

If huge, shining stars are difficult to see, how do scientists spot tiny, dark planets?

stars seen from Earth

powerful telescopes in Chile

How big is a planet compared to a star? Using a telescope, scientists can see Mercury pass by the Sun. The planet is a speck compared to the huge star!

Mercury

Sun

Planet Spotting

Scientists look at stars and planets using a powerful telescope called the Kepler Space Observatory.

In March 2009, Kepler was blasted into space.

Once there, it observed about 150,000 stars.

If a planet passed by one of the stars, it would block a tiny bit of the star's light.

Then Kepler would pick up and record the change in light.

A scientist prepares Kepler for launch.

The Kepler Space Observatory orbits the Sun while looking out into space.

Moon

Earth

Kepler is very good at spotting changes in light. It's like a person who can see a car's lights from miles away as well as a tiny bug walking across one of the headlamps!

11

Hunting for Exoplanets

Since its mission began, Kepler has detected thousands of planets.

These planets, which are outside our solar system, are known as **exoplanets**.

Kepler is looking for a special type of exoplanet—another Earth.

To be like Earth, the planet would need to be the perfect distance from its star.

Then, the exoplanet might have water—and life!

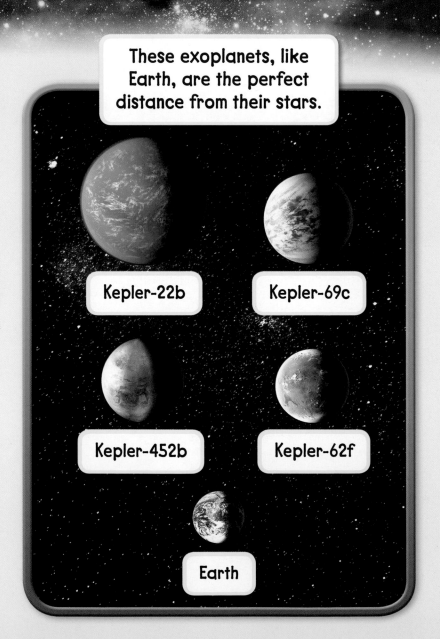

These exoplanets, like Earth, are the perfect distance from their stars.

Kepler-22b

Kepler-69c

Kepler-452b

Kepler-62f

Earth

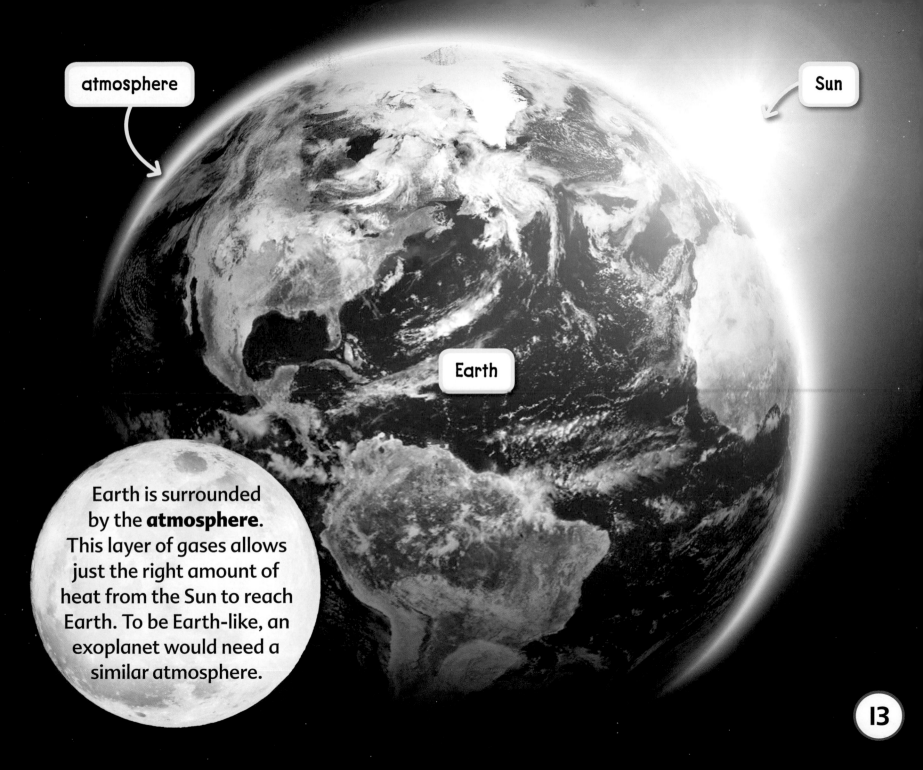

atmosphere

Sun

Earth

Earth is surrounded by the **atmosphere**. This layer of gases allows just the right amount of heat from the Sun to reach Earth. To be Earth-like, an exoplanet would need a similar atmosphere.

Another Earth?

In April 2014, scientists made an important discovery.

Kepler spotted a planet about the same size as Earth that may have water.

Scientists named it Kepler-186f.

For now, scientists can't find out more about the planet.

It's so far away it would take hundreds of thousands of years for humans to reach it!

In April 2018, another telescope was launched into space to hunt for exoplanets. Named TESS, it will observe over 200,000 stars.

TESS stands for "Transiting Exoplanet Survey Satellite."

By 2025, another powerful telescope will be launched into space.

The James Webb Space Telescope (JWST) will study the atmospheres of Earth-like exoplanets. Why?

The gases in a planet's atmosphere can tell scientists a lot.

For example, if an exoplanet's atmosphere contains oxygen, there could be living things on the planet!

scientists building the JWST

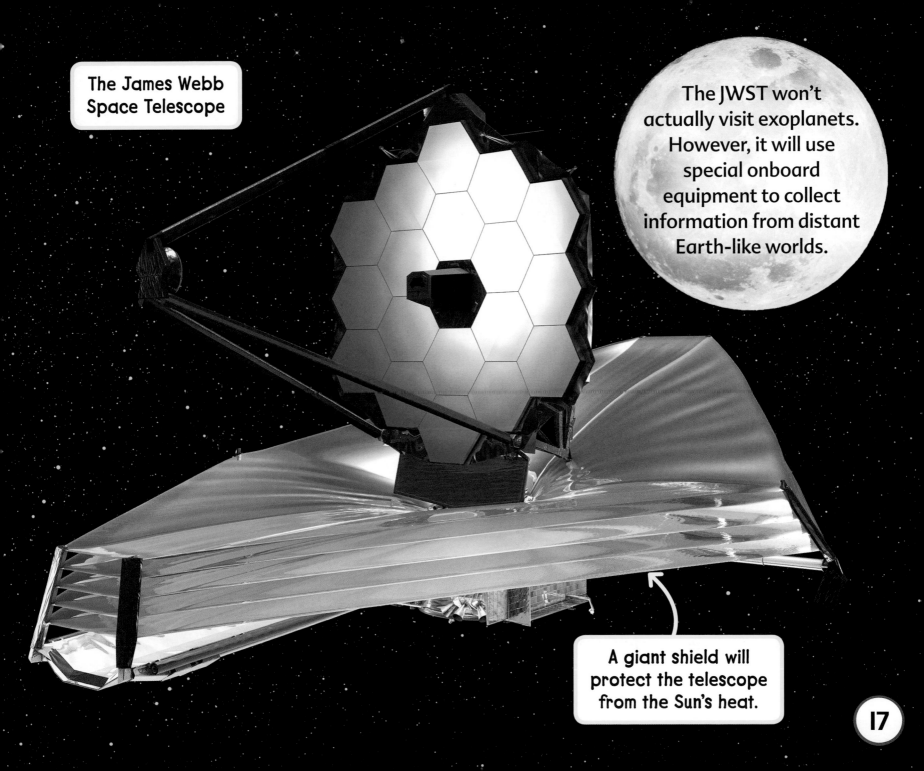

Visiting an Exoplanet

The closest known Earth-like exoplanet is called Proxima Centauri b.

However, it's still 25 trillion miles (40 trillion km) away from Earth.

It would take about 30,000 years to get there on our fastest spacecraft.

A group of scientists have a plan to visit Proxima Centauri b.

They're developing several tiny spacecraft that can be blasted to the faraway world!

Each tiny spacecraft will be about the size of a credit card. The plan is called Breakthrough Starshot.

Breakthrough Starshot spacecraft

Breakthrough Starshot

Each tiny spacecraft will be carried on a rocket into space.

Then, scientists on Earth will aim laser beams at the spacecraft.

The lasers will blast the spacecraft toward Proxima Centauri b at 134 million miles per hour (216 million km/h).

The high-speed spacecraft will reach the exoplanet in just 20 years.

Then, scientists hope they will finally get to see another Earth-like world.

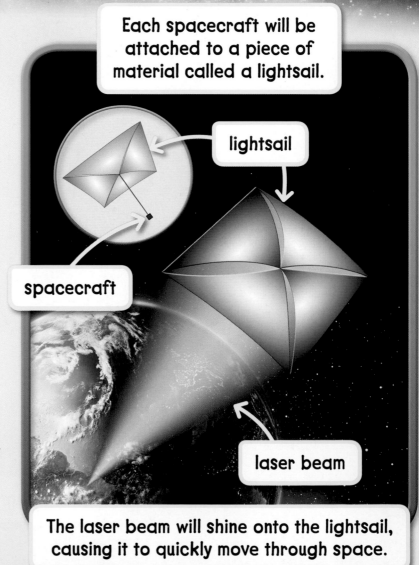

Each spacecraft will be attached to a piece of material called a lightsail.

lightsail

spacecraft

laser beam

The laser beam will shine onto the lightsail, causing it to quickly move through space.

When the spacecraft reach Proxima Centauri b, they will collect information and take photos. Then they will send their discoveries back to Earth.

This illustration shows what Proxima Centauri b might look like.

Imagine that scientists have sent a spacecraft to a distant Earth-like exoplanet. What would you want to know about the planet?

Science Lab

Build a Spacecraft!

Design your own tiny spacecraft to look for exoplanets.

You will need:
- Paper and colored pencils or paints
- Scissors
- Glue or tape
- Empty boxes, plastic bottles, toilet paper tubes, or other materials

1. Look at your materials and think of a design for your spacecraft.

2. Draw a picture of your design and label its parts.

3. Build a model of your spacecraft and give it a name.

Be a Scientist

Write a short report about your spacecraft, and answer the following questions:

- *What is your spacecraft's mission?*

- *What jobs do the different parts of your spacecraft do?*

- *What information will your spacecraft gather?*

Science Words

atmosphere (AT-muhss-fihr) the thick layer of gases surrounding Earth

exoplanets (EK-soh-plan-itz) planets that are outside of our solar system

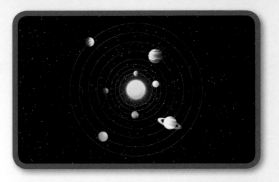

orbit (OR-bit) to circle, or move around, another object

planet (PLAN-et) a large, round object in space that is orbiting the Sun or another star

telescopes (TEL-uh-skohpz) scientific instruments used for seeing faraway objects

universe (YOO-nuh-vurss) everything that exists in space, including the stars and planets

Index

Read More

Kops, Deborah. *Exploring Exoplanets (Searchlight Books: What's Amazing About Space?).* Minneapolis, MN: Lerner (2012).

Lawrence, Ellen. *Earth: Our Home in the Solar System (Zoom Into Space).* New York: Ruby Tuesday (2014).

Lawrence, Ellen. *Surviving in Space (Space-ology).* New York: Bearport (2019).

Learn More Online

To learn more about exoplanets, visit
www.bearportpublishing.com/space-ology

About the Author

Ellen Lawrence lives in the United Kingdom and fully admits to being a huge space geek! While researching and writing this series, she loved watching interviews with astronauts and spine-tingling launch countdowns.

Answer for Page 7

It's called the "Goldilocks zone" after the fairy-tale character who was looking for a bowl of porridge that was not too hot and not too cold!